Title of the Book

"Social Media and Decision-Making: A New Paradigm"

By

Ms. Manpreet Kaur

Assistant-Professor

Chandigarh University,

Gharuan, Mohali

Introduction

- Overview of social media's rise and significance.
- The purpose of the book: to explore how social media influences decision-making.

Chapter 1: The Evolution of Communication

- Historical context of communication and decision-making.
- Transition from traditional media to social media.

Chapter 2: Understanding Decision-Making

- Definition and theories of decision-making.
- Factors influencing individual and group decisions.

Chapter 3: Social Media Dynamics

- How social media platforms function.
- The role of algorithms in shaping content exposure.

Chapter 4: Information Overload and Cognitive Biases

- The impact of excessive information on decision quality.
- Common cognitive biases amplified by social media.

Chapter 5: Peer Influence and Social Proof

- The concept of social proof in decision-making.
- Case studies of peer influence in consumer behaviour.

Chapter 6: The Role of Misinformation

- The prevalence of misinformation on social media.
- Effects of misinformation on public decisions and beliefs.

Chapter 7: Social Media in Political and Social Contexts

- How social media shapes political opinions and activism.
- The role of social media in social movements.

Chapter 8: Strategies for Effective Decision-Making

- Tips for individuals to navigate social media influence.
- How to critically evaluate information and sources.

Chapter 9: Future Trends in Social Media and Decision-Making

- Predictions for the evolution of social media and its impact on decision-making.
- The role of emerging technologies (e.g., AI, AR/VR) in shaping future decisions.

Conclusion

Appendices

References

- A comprehensive list of sources cited throughout the book.

Introduction

In the last two decades, social media has transformed the way we communicate, share information, and connect. Platforms like Facebook, Twitter, Instagram, and TikTok have not only revolutionized interpersonal interactions but have also reshaped entire industries, from marketing and journalism to politics and education. With billions of users globally, social media has emerged as a dominant force in shaping public discourse and influencing personal behaviours.

The significance of social media lies in its ability to democratize information sharing, allowing individuals to voice their opinions, share their experiences, and connect with like-minded communities. This unprecedented access to information and diverse perspectives has fundamentally altered how decisions are made at both individual and societal levels. In an age where a single tweet or post can spark global movements or influence consumer trends, understanding the dynamics of social media's impact on decision-making has never been more critical.

This book, **"Social Media and Decision-Making: A New Paradigm,"** aims to explore the intricate relationship between social media and the decision-making processes of individuals and groups. We will delve into how social media platforms function, the psychological mechanisms that drive user engagement, and the influence of social proof, peer pressure, and misinformation on our choices. By examining these aspects, we will uncover how social media shapes perceptions, attitudes, and ultimately, decisions across various contexts, including consumer behavior, political engagement, and social interactions.

As we navigate this complex digital landscape, it is essential to equip ourselves with the tools and insights needed to make informed decisions. This book seeks not only to highlight the challenges posed by social media's pervasive influence but also to offer strategies for harnessing its potential positively. By fostering a critical understanding of how social media impacts our decision-making, we can empower ourselves to navigate this new paradigm with awareness and intention.

Join us as we embark on this exploration of social media's profound effects on decision-making, paving the way for a deeper understanding of the choices we make in an increasingly connected world.

Chapter 1: The Evolution of Communication

Historical Context of Communication and Decision-Making

The evolution of communication is a narrative that spans centuries, reflecting humanity's ongoing quest for connection, understanding, and the dissemination of knowledge. From the earliest forms of verbal communication among small groups of people to the sophisticated digital dialogues of today, each stage in this evolution has had profound implications for how decisions are made.

1. **Oral Traditions and Early Communication**
In ancient societies, communication was primarily oral. Stories, knowledge, and cultural norms were passed down through generations via spoken word. This form of communication relied heavily on the credibility of the speaker and the shared context of the audience. Decisions in these early societies were often made collectively, with leaders or elders influencing the group based on their wisdom and experience. The communal nature of decision-making fostered a strong sense of belonging and trust within communities.

2. **The Invention of Writing**
The advent of writing marked a significant turning point in communication history. With the ability to record and transmit information in a more permanent form, societies could document laws, religious texts, and historical events. This shift allowed for more complex decision-making processes, as people could reference written texts to guide their choices. Writing also enabled the

rise of bureaucracy and formal institutions, changing how power and influence were distributed within societies.

3. The Printing Press

The invention of the printing press in the 15th century revolutionized communication once again. By making written materials more accessible, it democratized knowledge and empowered individuals to make informed decisions based on a broader range of information. The spread of pamphlets, books, and newspapers ignited social movements and fostered public discourse, allowing diverse voices to emerge and influence societal choices. This era saw the rise of the public sphere, where individuals could engage in discussions about politics, science, and culture.

4. Broadcast Media

The 20th century introduced radio and television, further transforming communication dynamics. These mediums allowed for the rapid dissemination of information to large audiences, shaping public opinion and influencing decision-making on a mass scale. News broadcasts, advertisements, and entertainment programs became critical tools for shaping societal norms and consumer behavior. The rise of mass media also led to the phenomenon of celebrity culture, where public figures could sway decisions and trends simply by sharing their views or endorsements.

Transition from Traditional Media to Social Media

The turn of the 21st century brought about the digital revolution, fundamentally altering the landscape of communication. The rise of the internet and social media platforms has created a paradigm shift in how information is created, shared, and consumed.

1. Emergence of the Internet

The internet's arrival provided a platform for instantaneous communication, enabling individuals to connect across geographical boundaries. Email, forums, and instant messaging facilitated conversations that transcended traditional barriers, allowing for the exchange of ideas and opinions at unprecedented speeds. The internet also introduced the concept of user-generated content, empowering individuals to contribute their voices to the collective narrative.

2. The Rise of Social Media

Social media platforms such as Facebook, Twitter, Instagram, and LinkedIn emerged, offering new ways for people to communicate and interact. Unlike traditional media, where information flowed from a few sources to many, social media allows for a decentralized flow of information. Users can create, share, and engage with content, fostering a participatory culture where every voice has the potential to be heard.

3. Shifting Decision-Making Dynamics

As social media took root, it began to influence decision-making processes in profound ways. Users are no longer passive consumers of information; they actively participate in discussions, share their experiences, and engage with others. This interactivity has shifted the power dynamics in decision-making, as individuals often seek validation and guidance from their social networks rather than relying solely on expert opinions or traditional authorities.

4. The Role of Algorithms

The algorithms that govern social media platforms curate content based on user behavior, preferences, and interactions. While this personalization enhances user experience, it can also create echo chambers, where individuals are exposed primarily to information that aligns with their existing beliefs. This phenomenon can significantly influence decision-making by reinforcing biases and limiting exposure to diverse perspectives.

5. A New Era of Communication

The transition from traditional media to social media represents a shift toward a more dynamic, interactive, and immediate form of communication. As users engage with one another and with content, decision-making becomes increasingly complex, influenced by factors such as peer pressure, social validation, and the rapid spread of information.

Conclusion

In summary, the evolution of communication from oral traditions to digital platforms has profoundly influenced how decisions are made. Each stage has brought new tools and dynamics that shape our understanding of information and its impact on our choices. As we move further into the age of social media, it is crucial to recognize the implications of this evolution on individual and collective decision-making processes, setting the stage for deeper exploration in the subsequent chapters of this book.

Chapter 2: Understanding Decision-Making

Definition and Theories of Decision-Making

1. Definition of Decision-Making

Decision-making is the cognitive process of selecting a course of action from among multiple alternatives. It involves identifying a decision point, gathering relevant information, evaluating options, and ultimately making a choice. This process can range from simple decisions, such as what to eat for lunch, to complex, high-stakes choices, like selecting a career path or making financial investments.

2. Theories of Decision-Making

Various theories have been developed to explain how individuals and groups make decisions. Some of the most prominent theories include:

- **Rational Choice Theory**: This theory posits that individuals make decisions by rationally evaluating options based on the maximization of personal benefit or utility. Decision-makers are assumed to have complete information and will weigh the costs and benefits of each alternative before arriving at a conclusion. However, this model often oversimplifies real-world decision-making, as it does not account for emotional factors or cognitive biases.

- **Bounded Rationality**: Introduced by Herbert Simon, this theory acknowledges that while individuals strive to make rational choices, their ability to do so is limited by cognitive constraints, lack of information, and time pressures. As a result, decision-makers often settle for "satisficing," choosing the first option that meets their criteria rather than the optimal solution.
- **Prospect Theory**: Developed by Daniel Kahneman and Amos Tversky, prospect theory describes how people evaluate potential losses and gains when making decisions under uncertainty. It highlights that individuals are generally more sensitive to potential losses than equivalent gains, leading them to make risk-averse choices in the face of loss.
- **Heuristics and Biases**: This approach focuses on the mental shortcuts (heuristics) individuals use to simplify decision-making. While heuristics can be efficient, they can also lead to systematic biases, such as overconfidence, anchoring (relying too heavily on the first piece of information encountered), and availability bias (overestimating the importance of information that is readily available).
- **Social Decision-Making Theories**: These theories emphasize the influence of social dynamics in decision-making processes. Concepts like social proof (the tendency to conform to the behavior of others) and groupthink (the tendency for cohesive groups to prioritize consensus over critical analysis) highlight how individual decisions can be shaped by group interactions and societal norms.

Factors Influencing Individual and Group Decisions

Decision-making is influenced by a multitude of factors that can vary significantly depending on whether the decision is made individually or collectively. Here are some key factors that play a role in both contexts:

1. Cognitive Factors

- **Information Processing**: The way individuals process information affects their decisions. Factors such as cognitive overload can hinder effective evaluation of options.
- **Cognitive Biases**: As previously mentioned, biases can lead to errors in judgment and influence choices in various contexts.

2. Emotional Factors

- **Emotions and Mood**: Emotions can significantly influence decision-making, with positive moods often leading to riskier choices and negative moods prompting more conservative decisions.
- **Fear and Anxiety**: These emotions can lead to avoidance behaviors, impacting the willingness to make certain decisions.

3. Social Influences

- **Peer Pressure**: Social dynamics play a crucial role, with individuals often swayed by the opinions and behaviors of their peers.
- **Cultural Norms**: Cultural background shapes values and beliefs, influencing how decisions are approached and prioritized.

4. Contextual Factors

- **Situational Context**: The context in which a decision is made—such as time constraints, environmental factors, and available resources—can impact the decision-making process.
- **Risk Perception**: Individuals assess risk differently based on their experiences and the context of the decision, affecting their willingness to take risks.

5. Group Dynamics

- **Group Size and Composition**: The size and diversity of a group can influence the decision-making process, with larger groups sometimes leading to diffusion of responsibility and decreased accountability.
- **Leadership Styles**: The approach taken by leaders can shape group dynamics and influence how decisions are made and accepted within the group.

6. Social Media Influence

- **Information Flow**: The speed and volume of information available on social media can impact decision-making processes. Individuals may rely on social media to seek validation, gather opinions, or compare choices with their networks.
- **Echo Chambers**: Social media can create environments where individuals are exposed primarily to viewpoints that align with their own, reinforcing existing beliefs and biases.

Conclusion

Understanding decision-making is essential for navigating the complexities of modern life, especially in an era dominated by social media. By exploring the various theories of decision-making and the factors that influence choices, we gain valuable insights into how individuals and groups arrive at decisions. This foundational knowledge sets the stage for further exploration of how social media intersects with decision-making processes, shaping our choices in profound ways. As we move forward in this book, we will delve deeper into the specific impacts of social media on decision-making, revealing the opportunities and challenges it presents.

Chapter 3: Social Media Dynamics

How Social Media Platforms Function

Social media platforms are digital spaces that facilitate the creation, sharing, and exchange of user-generated content. These platforms are designed to enable users to connect, interact, and communicate with one another in real time. Understanding how these platforms function is crucial for comprehending their influence on decision-making.

1. User Profiles and Networking

Users create personal profiles that showcase their identities, interests, and activities. These profiles allow individuals to connect with friends, family, and like-minded people, forming a network of relationships. The strength and composition of these networks play a vital role in shaping the information users are exposed to and the decisions they make.

2. Content Creation and Sharing

Social media platforms provide various tools for users to create and share content, including text posts, images, videos, and live streams. This user-generated content is a key feature that differentiates social media from traditional media, where content is typically created by professionals or organizations. The ability to share personal experiences, opinions, and recommendations empowers users to influence one another's decisions.

3. Interaction and Engagement

Users can interact with content through likes, comments, shares, and reactions. This engagement fosters a sense of community and encourages discussions around specific topics. The level of interaction on a post can amplify its visibility, leading to a feedback loop where popular content reaches even wider audiences. Engagement metrics serve as indicators of content popularity, influencing what users see in their feeds.

4. Community Building

Social media platforms enable the formation of communities based on shared interests, values, or experiences. These communities can provide support, information, and a sense of belonging. For instance, groups focused on health, hobbies, or political activism can influence members' decisions by providing collective knowledge and experiences.

5. Diverse Content Formats

Platforms support a wide array of content formats, including articles, images, videos, polls, and stories. This diversity caters to different user preferences and enhances the overall experience. By providing various ways to engage with information, social media can influence users' perceptions and decision-making processes in unique ways.

The Role of Algorithms in Shaping Content Exposure

Algorithms play a crucial role in determining the content users see on social media platforms. These algorithms analyze user behavior, preferences, and interactions to curate personalized content feeds. Understanding how algorithms function is essential for recognizing their impact on decision-making.

1. Data Collection and User Behavior

Social media platforms collect vast amounts of data on user behavior, including likes, shares, comments, and browsing history. This data is used to create profiles of users' interests and preferences. The more a user interacts with certain types of content, the more tailored their feed becomes, as the algorithm learns which posts are most engaging for them.

2. Personalization of Content

Algorithms prioritize content based on relevance to the individual user. Factors such as engagement history, the relationships a user has with other accounts, and the timing of posts all influence what appears in a user's feed. This personalization enhances user experience by delivering content that aligns with their interests, but it can also lead to echo chambers where users are primarily exposed to viewpoints that reinforce their existing beliefs.

3. Content Ranking

Social media algorithms employ ranking systems to determine which posts are displayed prominently. This ranking is based on various criteria, including:

- **Engagement Metrics**: Posts that receive high levels of interaction are prioritized, leading to increased visibility.
- **Recency**: Newer posts may be favored to keep content fresh and relevant.
- **Relevance**: Content that aligns closely with a user's interests is likely to be shown more frequently.

4. Promotion of Trending Topics

Algorithms can identify trending topics and popular content across the platform, promoting them to a broader audience. This feature can create viral trends that influence public opinion and behavior. For instance, challenges, hashtags, and viral videos can rapidly spread across networks, impacting collective decision-making in areas such as consumer behavior and social movements.

5. Impact on Information Diversity

While algorithms enhance personalization, they can also limit the diversity of information users encounter. When users are primarily shown content that aligns with their preferences, they may miss out on alternative viewpoints or critical information. This phenomenon can contribute to polarization, where individuals become entrenched in their beliefs and are less open to differing perspectives.

6. Algorithmic Transparency and Ethics

The opacity of social media algorithms raises ethical concerns regarding manipulation and control of information. Users may be unaware of how their content exposure is shaped, leading to questions about agency and responsibility. Discussions around algorithmic transparency are increasingly important, as society grapples with the implications of algorithm-driven decision-making.

Conclusion

Social media platforms function as dynamic environments that facilitate communication, content sharing, and community building. Algorithms play a pivotal role in shaping users' experiences by personalizing content exposure and influencing engagement. As we navigate these platforms, it is essential to recognize the implications of these dynamics on decision-making processes. The next chapters will further explore how social media influences individual and group decisions, highlighting the opportunities and challenges posed by this new digital landscape.

Chapter 4: Information Overload and Cognitive Biases

The Impact of Excessive Information on Decision Quality

In the age of social media, individuals are inundated with vast amounts of information on a daily basis. This phenomenon, often referred to as **information overload**, can have profound effects on decision quality.

1. **Definition of Information Overload**

Information overload occurs when the amount of available information exceeds an individual's processing capacity, leading to feelings of confusion, frustration, and indecision. As social media platforms facilitate the rapid sharing of content, users are bombarded with news articles, posts, videos, and opinions, making it increasingly challenging to discern valuable information from noise.

2. Effects on Decision Quality

- **Reduced Clarity**: The sheer volume of information can obscure critical insights, making it difficult for individuals to identify relevant factors influencing their decisions. This lack of clarity can lead to poor decision-making, as users may rely on incomplete or misleading information.

- **Analysis Paralysis**: Faced with too many options or too much information, individuals may experience analysis paralysis, where they become overwhelmed and struggle to make a choice. This can result in procrastination or avoidance of decision-making altogether.
- **Increased Stress and Anxiety**: The pressure to keep up with a constant stream of information can lead to stress and anxiety, further impairing cognitive functioning. Emotional distress can cloud judgment, leading to impulsive or irrational decisions.
- **Difficulty in Prioritization**: Information overload can hinder individuals' ability to prioritize, as they may struggle to distinguish between what is essential and what is trivial. This can result in focusing on less relevant factors while overlooking more critical ones.
- **Impact on Trust and Credibility**: In an environment flooded with information, distinguishing credible sources from unreliable ones becomes challenging. Users may struggle to determine which information is trustworthy, leading to a reliance on hearsay or popular opinion rather than factual evidence.

Common Cognitive Biases Amplified by Social Media

Cognitive biases are systematic errors in thinking that can distort judgment and decision-making. Social media, with its unique dynamics, can exacerbate these biases in various ways:

1. Confirmation Bias

Confirmation bias refers to the tendency to search for, interpret, and remember information in a way that confirms one's preexisting beliefs. Social media can reinforce this bias by curating content that aligns with users' interests, leading them to engage with information that supports their views while ignoring contradictory evidence.

2. Bandwagon Effect

The bandwagon effect occurs when individuals adopt beliefs or behaviors because they perceive that others are doing so. On social media, trending topics and viral posts can create a sense of social proof, leading users to make decisions based on popularity rather than personal conviction. This effect can significantly impact opinions on political issues, consumer products, and social movements.

3. Availability Heuristic

The availability heuristic is the mental shortcut that relies on immediate examples that come to mind when evaluating a decision. Social media amplifies this bias by making certain events or information more visible and memorable. For instance, if a particular issue is frequently discussed or shared, individuals may overestimate its prevalence or importance, influencing their decisions accordingly.

4. Overconfidence Bias

Overconfidence bias occurs when individuals overestimate their knowledge or abilities. In the context of social media, users may feel overly confident in their understanding of complex issues based on limited information or anecdotal evidence. This can lead to misguided decisions, as individuals may ignore expert advice or relevant data.

5. Negativity Bias

Negativity bias refers to the tendency to give more weight to negative experiences or information than positive ones. On social media, negative news stories or critical comments can garner significant attention, influencing public perception and decision-making. This bias can lead individuals to be overly cautious or fearful, impacting their choices and actions.

6. Echo Chamber Effect

The echo chamber effect occurs when individuals are exposed primarily to information that reinforces their existing beliefs, leading to a lack of exposure to diverse perspectives. Social media algorithms often create echo chambers by promoting content that aligns with users' interests. This effect can lead to polarization and a diminished capacity for critical thinking, as individuals may become entrenched in their views and less open to differing opinions.

Conclusion

Information overload and cognitive biases are significant challenges in the decision-making landscape shaped by social media. The excessive volume of information can impair decision quality, leading to confusion and stress, while cognitive biases can distort judgment and reinforce preexisting beliefs. As we navigate this complex digital environment, it is essential to develop strategies for managing information effectively and recognizing the influence of biases on our decisions. In the following chapters, we will explore how social media impacts decision-making in various contexts, revealing both the opportunities and challenges it presents.

Chapter 5: Peer Influence and Social Proof

The Concept of Social Proof in Decision-Making

Social proof is a psychological phenomenon where individuals look to the behaviours and opinions of others to guide their own decisions, particularly in situations of uncertainty. This concept is grounded in the idea that people often rely on the collective wisdom of their peers to determine what is appropriate or effective, especially when they lack sufficient information.

1. **Types of Social Proof**

Social proof can take various forms, including:

- **Expert Social Proof**: Endorsements or recommendations from recognized authorities or experts in a particular field. For example, a product recommended by a well-known influencer or expert can enhance its credibility and influence consumer choices.
- **User Social Proof**: Testimonials, reviews, and ratings from other consumers. Positive reviews on platforms like Amazon or Yelp can significantly impact purchasing decisions, as potential buyers perceive them as indicators of quality and reliability.

- **Crowd Social Proof**: The behavior of large groups of people can signal what is considered acceptable or desirable. For instance, long lines outside a restaurant can suggest that it is worth trying, leading more people to join the queue.
- **Wisdom of the Crowd**: The aggregated opinions or decisions of a group can often lead to accurate judgments. For example, crowdsourcing platforms like Kickstarter rely on collective feedback to gauge the viability of new ideas or products.

2. **Mechanisms Behind Social Proof**

Several psychological mechanisms underpin social proof, including:

- **Uncertainty Reduction**: In unfamiliar situations, individuals seek cues from others to reduce uncertainty. Observing what others do can provide guidance on how to act.
- **Conformity**: The desire to fit in or be accepted by a group can drive individuals to align their decisions with those of their peers.
- **Trust in Collective Judgment**: People often believe that if many others are making a particular choice, it must be a valid or wise decision. This reliance on collective judgment can lead to herd behavior, where individuals follow the crowd, sometimes to the detriment of their own interests.

Case Studies of Peer Influence in Consumer Behavior

Understanding the impact of peer influence and social proof on consumer behavior is essential for recognizing how decisions are shaped in the social media landscape. The following case studies illustrate the profound effect of social proof on purchasing decisions.

1. The Ice Bucket Challenge

The Ice Bucket Challenge, which went viral in 2014, was a fundraising campaign for ALS (Amyotrophic Lateral Sclerosis) research. Participants would pour a bucket of ice water over themselves and challenge others to do the same while donating to the cause. The campaign's rapid spread on social media showcased the power of peer influence; as celebrities and friends participated, others felt compelled to join in. The social proof created by widespread participation not only raised awareness but also generated significant financial contributions, illustrating how collective action can drive consumer behavior in support of a cause.

2. Fashion and Social Media Influencers

Social media influencers play a crucial role in shaping fashion trends and consumer preferences. When influencers showcase clothing or accessories, their followers often perceive these endorsements as social proof. For example, when a popular influencer posts a photo wearing a specific brand, it can lead to increased sales for that brand. A case in point is the rise of fast fashion retailers like PrettyLittleThing and Fashion Nova, which thrive on influencer marketing. The social proof generated by influencers wearing their products creates a sense of desirability, driving followers to make similar purchases.

3. Yelp Reviews and Restaurant Choices

Yelp, a platform that allows users to rate and review businesses, has become a vital tool for consumers seeking dining options. Studies have shown that restaurants with higher ratings and positive reviews on Yelp experience increased foot traffic and sales. Consumers often rely on the social proof of others' experiences to make dining decisions, particularly in unfamiliar areas. A case study of a new restaurant in a competitive market revealed that positive Yelp reviews led to a substantial increase in patronage, demonstrating how social proof can influence consumer choices in the hospitality industry.

4. Amazon Ratings and Product Choices

On e-commerce platforms like Amazon, product ratings and reviews serve as powerful forms of social proof. A study found that products with a higher number of positive reviews are more likely to be purchased. For instance, an analysis of a popular tech gadget revealed that when the product's rating increased from three to four stars, sales nearly doubled. Consumers are more likely to trust products that have been positively evaluated by others, illustrating how social proof directly impacts purchasing behavior in online retail.

5. Travel Recommendations on Social Media

Social media platforms like Instagram and Facebook have transformed how people plan their travel. Users often seek recommendations from friends, family, and influencers, relying on social proof to guide their choices. For example, a travel-related Instagram post showcasing a picturesque destination can spark interest among followers, leading them to consider that location for their next trip. Research indicates that travelers are more likely to choose destinations that have been recommended by peers, highlighting the role of social proof in influencing travel decisions.

Conclusion

Peer influence and social proof are powerful drivers of decision-making in the social media landscape. By understanding how social proof operates and its effects on consumer behavior, individuals can become more mindful of the external influences shaping their choices. As we continue to explore the intersection of social media and decision-making, it is essential to recognize the role of peer dynamics and collective behaviors in shaping our preferences and actions. The following chapters will delve deeper into the implications of social media for decision-making in various contexts, including political engagement and social movements.

Chapter 6: The Role of Misinformation

The Prevalence of Misinformation on Social Media

In the digital age, social media platforms have become fertile ground for the rapid spread of misinformation. Misinformation refers to false or misleading information that is shared, regardless of intent. This phenomenon poses significant challenges to informed decision-making and public discourse.

1. **Characteristics of Misinformation**

Misinformation can take various forms, including:

- **False Information**: Completely fabricated content presented as factual, such as fake news articles.
- **Misleading Information**: Information that distorts the truth or presents facts out of context, leading to misinterpretation.
- **Disinformation**: Deliberately misleading or biased information shared with the intent to deceive, often associated with political agendas.

2. Mechanisms of Spread

Several factors contribute to the prevalence of misinformation on social media:

- **Viral Nature of Content**: Social media's design encourages the rapid sharing of posts, making it easy for misinformation to go viral. Engaging headlines or shocking claims often attract attention, leading users to share content without verifying its accuracy.
- **Algorithmic Amplification**: Social media algorithms prioritize content that generates high engagement, often promoting sensational or controversial posts. This can result in the widespread dissemination of misinformation as it captures user interest.
- **Echo Chambers**: Social media users often gravitate towards communities that reinforce their beliefs, creating echo chambers where misinformation can thrive. Within these environments, false claims may circulate unchallenged, further entrenching users in their beliefs.

3. Notable Examples of Misinformation

High-profile cases of misinformation have drawn attention to its prevalence on social media. For instance:

- **COVID-19 Misinformation**: During the pandemic, false claims about the virus, its origins, and treatments circulated widely on social media, complicating public health efforts and influencing behavior.
- **Election Misinformation**: In the lead-up to elections, misinformation about voting processes, candidates, and political parties has been rampant, impacting voter perceptions and participation.

Effects of Misinformation on Public Decisions and Beliefs

The proliferation of misinformation has significant consequences for public decision-making and belief systems, affecting various aspects of society.

1. Erosion of Trust in Institutions

- **Declining Trust in Media and Experts**: Misinformation can undermine public trust in traditional media sources and experts. When false claims proliferate, people may become skeptical of legitimate news outlets and professionals, leading to a culture of distrust that complicates efforts to disseminate accurate information.
- **Polarization**: Misinformation can exacerbate societal divisions, as individuals may gravitate towards sources that align with their beliefs. This polarization can create an environment where differing viewpoints are dismissed, further entrenching misinformation.

2. Impact on Health Decisions

- **Public Health Risks**: Misinformation surrounding health topics can lead to harmful decisions. For example, during the COVID-19 pandemic, misinformation about vaccine efficacy and safety influenced public attitudes, resulting in vaccine hesitancy and lower vaccination rates.
- **Alternative Treatments**: Misinformation about alternative treatments can mislead individuals into choosing ineffective or harmful health practices. This can have serious implications for individual and public health.

3. Influence on Political Decisions

- **Voter Behavior**: Misinformation can significantly impact voter behavior and perceptions of candidates. False claims about candidates or policies can shape public opinion, potentially influencing election outcomes.
- **Erosion of Democratic Processes**: Widespread misinformation can undermine democratic processes by creating confusion around voting procedures, which may discourage participation or lead to voter apathy.

4. Challenges to Critical Thinking

- **Reduced Media Literacy**: The prevalence of misinformation underscores the importance of media literacy. As individuals encounter false information, the ability to critically evaluate sources and claims becomes increasingly crucial. However, many users lack the skills necessary to navigate the complex information landscape, leading to reliance on unverified sources.
- **Cognitive Overload**: Faced with a constant barrage of information, including misinformation, individuals may struggle to discern credible content from false claims. This cognitive overload can hinder effective decision-making, as users may resort to heuristics or emotional responses rather than rational analysis.

5. Societal Implications

- **Influence on Social Movements**: Misinformation can shape public perception and action within social movements. False narratives can either bolster or undermine the legitimacy of causes, impacting participation and support.

- **Potential for Conflict**: The spread of misinformation can escalate tensions within communities, leading to conflict and division. Misunderstandings fueled by false information can create animosity among different groups, further complicating efforts to address social issues.

Conclusion

Misinformation poses a significant threat to informed decision-making in the age of social media. The prevalence of false information, combined with the mechanisms that facilitate its spread, has far-reaching effects on public beliefs and behaviors. As individuals navigate this complex information landscape, fostering critical thinking and media literacy becomes essential. In the following chapters, we will explore strategies for combating misinformation and promoting accurate information in decision-making processes, as well as the role of social media in facilitating informed public discourse.

Chapter 7: Social Media in Political and Social Contexts

How Social Media Shapes Political Opinions and Activism

Social media has fundamentally transformed the political landscape by influencing how individuals form opinions and engage with political issues. Its capacity to facilitate communication, mobilize communities, and amplify voices has made it an essential tool for both politicians and citizens.

1. Information Dissemination

Social media platforms serve as primary channels for political communication. Politicians, parties, and advocacy groups utilize social media to share their messages directly with the public. This direct communication can lead to:

- **Rapid Information Spread**: News about political events, policy changes, and election updates can be disseminated almost instantaneously, allowing users to stay informed in real-time.
- **Increased Accessibility**: Social media lowers barriers to entry for political engagement, enabling individuals to access information and participate in discussions that might have been difficult to reach through traditional media outlets.

2. Influencing Political Opinions

Social media plays a crucial role in shaping political opinions through several mechanisms:

- **Echo Chambers**: Users often engage with content that aligns with their beliefs, creating echo chambers that reinforce existing opinions. This can limit exposure to diverse viewpoints and contribute to polarization.
- **Influencer Impact**: Social media influencers and thought leaders can sway public opinion on political issues by leveraging their platforms to advocate for specific causes or candidates. Their endorsements can significantly influence their followers' views.
- **Real-Time Feedback**: Politicians can gauge public sentiment through social media interactions, allowing them to adjust their messages and policies in response to voter reactions. This immediacy can enhance political responsiveness but may also lead to populism, where decisions are driven more by social media trends than by informed policy considerations.

3. Grassroots Activism and Mobilization

Social media empowers grassroots movements by providing a platform for organizing and mobilizing supporters. Key aspects include:

- **Event Organization**: Activists can quickly organize events, rallies, and protests through social media, reaching a broad audience and encouraging participation. Platforms like Facebook and Twitter have facilitated the coordination of large-scale protests.
- **Community Building**: Social media fosters connections among individuals with shared interests, allowing grassroots organizations to build supportive communities. These connections can amplify the impact of social movements and foster collaboration.

- **Fundraising and Resource Sharing**: Social media allows activists to raise funds and share resources efficiently. Crowdfunding campaigns for political causes or social justice initiatives have gained traction through platforms like GoFundMe and Kickstarter.

The Role of Social Media in Social Movements

Social media has played a transformative role in the emergence and success of various social movements. By providing a platform for marginalized voices and enabling widespread mobilization, social media has reshaped the dynamics of activism.

1. **Amplifying Marginalized Voices**

Social media has democratized the conversation around social justice, allowing individuals and communities that have historically been silenced to share their stories and advocate for change. Key movements have leveraged social media to:

- **Raise Awareness**: Hashtags like #BlackLivesMatter and #MeToo have become rallying cries, drawing attention to systemic injustices and mobilizing support for reform. These movements have generated global conversations about race, gender, and equity.
- **Showcase Personal Narratives**: Individuals can share personal experiences and testimonies, humanizing social issues and fostering empathy. This storytelling aspect has been crucial in shifting public perception and understanding.

2. **Facilitating Global Solidarity**

Social media allows for the formation of transnational networks of solidarity. Movements can gain international support and visibility, leading to increased pressure on governments and institutions. Examples include:

- **Arab Spring**: Social media played a pivotal role in the Arab Spring protests, enabling activists to share information, coordinate actions, and garner international support for democratic movements across the Middle East and North Africa.
- **Climate Strikes**: Initiatives like Fridays for Future, inspired by Greta Thunberg, have gained global traction through social media. The movement encourages youth activism around climate change, showcasing the power of collective action across borders.

3. Challenges and Limitations

While social media has facilitated significant advances in activism, it also presents challenges:

- **Trolling and Harassment**: Activists often face online harassment and threats, which can deter participation and undermine the effectiveness of movements. The anonymity of social media can embolden individuals to engage in harmful behaviors.
- **Fragmentation of Movements**: The ease of creating groups and networks can lead to fragmentation within movements. Different factions may emerge, each with its own goals and strategies, complicating collective action and diluting impact.
- **Superficial Engagement**: The phenomenon of "slacktivism" describes a situation where individuals engage in low-effort actions (like sharing a post) without committing to meaningful activism. While social media can raise awareness, it may also create a false sense of accomplishment, leading to inaction.

Conclusion

Social media has become a powerful tool for shaping political opinions and facilitating social movements. By democratizing access to information and enabling grassroots activism, it has transformed the political landscape. However, the challenges associated with misinformation, echo chambers, and online harassment must be addressed to harness the full potential of social media for positive change. In the following chapters, we will explore strategies for leveraging social media effectively in decision-making processes and the implications of these developments for future societal trends.

Chapter 8: Strategies for Effective Decision-Making

As social media continues to shape the way we receive information and make decisions, it is essential to develop strategies that help individuals navigate this complex landscape. This chapter offers practical tips for effectively managing social media influence and critically evaluating information and sources.

Tips for Individuals to Navigate Social Media Influence

1. Be Mindful of Your Social Media Use

- **Limit Exposure**: Consider reducing the time spent on social media platforms. Set boundaries for daily usage and take breaks to avoid information overload. This can help mitigate the impact of social media on your decision-making processes.
- **Curate Your Feed**: Follow accounts and pages that provide balanced, credible information. Unfollow or mute sources that promote sensationalism, misinformation, or extreme viewpoints to create a more informative social media environment.

2. Diversify Your Sources of Information

- **Seek Out Multiple Perspectives**: Relying on a single source can limit your understanding of complex issues. Diversify your news sources by following outlets with different viewpoints. This can help you form a more nuanced perspective on the topics you care about.
- **Engage with Experts**: Follow credible experts in relevant fields on social media. Their insights can provide valuable context and enhance your understanding of specific issues.

3. Practice Active Engagement

- **Engage Thoughtfully**: Rather than passively scrolling through content, actively engage with posts by asking questions or seeking clarification. This encourages deeper thinking about the information presented and helps combat the effects of echo chambers.
- **Participate in Constructive Discussions**: Engage in conversations that promote dialogue and understanding. Respectful discussions with others can provide new insights and challenge your assumptions.

4. Develop Emotional Awareness

- **Recognize Emotional Triggers**: Be aware of how certain posts or topics make you feel. Emotional reactions can cloud judgment and lead to impulsive decisions. Take a step back if you find yourself reacting strongly to a post, and consider the information more objectively.
- **Pause Before Sharing**: Before sharing information or opinions, take a moment to reflect on its accuracy and potential impact. This pause can help prevent the spread of misinformation and encourage thoughtful engagement.

How to Critically Evaluate Information and Sources

To make informed decisions in the age of social media, it is crucial to develop strong critical thinking skills. Here are strategies for evaluating information and sources effectively:

1. Check the Source

- **Identify Credibility**: Research the source of the information. Established news organizations, academic institutions, and government agencies generally provide reliable information. Be cautious with anonymous sources or websites that lack transparency.
- **Look for Author Expertise**: Investigate the credentials and background of the author. Experts in their fields are more likely to provide accurate information based on research and experience.

2. Verify Facts and Claims

- **Cross-Reference Information**: When encountering new information, cross-check it with multiple reputable sources. If the claim is true, it should be corroborated by other credible outlets.
- **Use Fact-Checking Websites**: Utilize fact-checking organizations like Snopes, FactCheck.org, or PolitiFact to verify claims and debunk misinformation. These resources can help confirm the accuracy of information before sharing it.

3. Analyze the Content

- **Assess the Tone and Language**: Pay attention to the language used in the post or article. Sensationalist language, exaggerations, or emotionally charged words can be indicators of bias or misinformation.
- **Examine the Evidence**: Check whether the claims are supported by data, studies, or credible testimonials. Look for citations and references to reputable sources that lend credibility to the information presented.

4. Recognize Bias

- **Identify Potential Bias**: Consider the potential biases of the source and author. All sources may have some level of bias, whether intentional or unintentional. Being aware of these biases can help you evaluate the information more critically.
- **Be Wary of Confirmation Bias**: Challenge your own biases by seeking information that contradicts your beliefs. Engaging with differing perspectives can provide a more comprehensive understanding of complex issues.

5. Question the Motivation

- **Consider the Purpose**: Reflect on why the information is being shared. Is it to inform, persuade, provoke outrage, or entertain? Understanding the intent behind the content can help you evaluate its credibility and relevance.
- **Examine the Audience**: Analyze who the target audience is for the information. Posts aimed at generating outrage or fear may be designed to manipulate emotions rather than convey factual information.

Conclusion

In an era where social media plays a significant role in shaping opinions and decisions, developing effective strategies for navigating its influence is crucial. By practicing mindfulness, diversifying information sources, and critically evaluating the content encountered online, individuals can enhance their decision-making processes. These skills empower users to engage thoughtfully with the information they encounter, fostering a more informed and engaged society. In the final chapters, we will explore the future implications of social media on decision-making and strategies for fostering a healthier digital environment.

Chapter 9: Future Trends in Social Media and Decision-Making

As social media continues to evolve, it will significantly impact how individuals and organizations make decisions. This chapter explores predictions for the future of social media and its implications for decision-making, as well as the role of emerging technologies such as artificial intelligence (AI) and augmented/virtual reality (AR/VR) in shaping future choices.

Predictions for the Evolution of Social Media and Its Impact on Decision-Making

1. Increasing Personalization of Content

- **Tailored Experiences**: Future social media platforms are likely to use advanced algorithms to provide highly personalized content based on users' preferences, behaviors, and interests. This increased personalization will create more engaging user experiences but may also exacerbate echo chambers, where users are only exposed to information that reinforces their existing beliefs.
- **Influence on Decision-Making**: As content becomes more tailored, individuals may find it increasingly challenging to encounter diverse perspectives. This could lead to more polarized decision-making, as users are less likely to engage with conflicting viewpoints.

2. Shift Toward Authenticity and Transparency

- **Demand for Trustworthy Sources**: In response to the rise of misinformation, users may increasingly prioritize authenticity and transparency in the content they consume. This shift could prompt social media platforms to implement stricter verification processes for sources and content.

- **User-Generated Content**: As users seek more genuine interactions, platforms may promote user-generated content over professionally curated material. This could enhance community engagement and lead to more grassroots-driven decision-making processes.

3. Integration of Social Commerce

- **Seamless Shopping Experiences**: Social media platforms are likely to further integrate e-commerce features, allowing users to shop directly from posts and stories. This integration will streamline the purchasing process and influence consumer decisions through social proof and targeted advertising.
- **Impact on Consumer Behavior**: As social commerce becomes more prevalent, individuals may rely on social media recommendations and peer reviews more than ever when making purchasing decisions, reinforcing the importance of social proof in consumer behavior.

4. Enhanced Regulation and Policy Changes

- **Stricter Content Regulations**: In response to growing concerns about misinformation, privacy, and data security, governments and regulatory bodies may impose stricter regulations on social media platforms. These regulations could require greater accountability for the dissemination of information and the protection of user data.
- **Influence on User Trust**: Enhanced regulations may improve user trust in social media platforms, as users become more confident that the information they encounter is accurate and that their data is protected. This trust could lead to more meaningful engagement and informed decision-making.

The Role of Emerging Technologies in Shaping Future Decisions

1. Artificial Intelligence (AI)

- **Enhanced Content Curation**: AI will play a pivotal role in curating content for users, allowing for real-time analysis of user preferences and behaviors. Advanced algorithms will identify trends and tailor information to individual users, influencing their decisions based on data-driven insights.
- **Chatbots and Virtual Assistants**: The integration of AI-powered chatbots and virtual assistants on social media platforms will facilitate decision-making by providing users with instant access to information and recommendations. These tools can help users navigate complex choices, from purchasing decisions to health inquiries.

2. Augmented Reality (AR) and Virtual Reality (VR)

- **Immersive Experiences**: AR and VR technologies will create immersive social media experiences that allow users to visualize products and services before making decisions. For example, users might try on clothes virtually or visualize furniture in their homes through AR applications, enhancing their purchasing confidence.
- **Impact on Social Interactions**: As AR and VR become more integrated into social media, users will engage in new forms of social interactions, potentially reshaping how decisions are made in social contexts. Virtual gatherings, events, and experiences could enhance community building and collaborative decision-making.

3. Data Analytics and Decision-Making

- **Predictive Analytics**: Social media platforms will increasingly leverage data analytics to predict user behaviors and preferences. By analyzing vast amounts of user data, platforms can anticipate trends and tailor recommendations accordingly, shaping individual and collective decision-making processes.
- **Informed Public Discourse**: Enhanced data analytics can provide valuable insights into public sentiment on various issues, allowing organizations and policymakers to make more informed decisions. This can lead to more responsive governance and better alignment with community needs.

4. Ethical Considerations and Responsibility

- **Navigating Ethical Challenges**: As technologies evolve, ethical considerations regarding privacy, data security, and user manipulation will become increasingly important. Social media platforms must navigate these challenges responsibly to maintain user trust and ensure informed decision-making.
- **Fostering Digital Literacy**: The future of decision-making will depend on users' ability to critically evaluate information and engage with emerging technologies. Promoting digital literacy will be essential to empower individuals to make informed choices in a rapidly changing landscape.

Conclusion

The future of social media and its impact on decision-making is marked by rapid evolution and technological advancement. While emerging technologies like AI and AR/VR promise to enhance user experiences and streamline decision processes, they also present challenges related to misinformation, polarization, and ethical considerations. As individuals navigate this complex landscape, fostering critical thinking, digital literacy, and ethical awareness will be crucial to making informed decisions. In the concluding chapter, we will summarize the key insights from this book and discuss the implications of social media on decision-making for individuals and society as a whole.

Conclusion

In an age where social media is deeply embedded in our daily lives, its influence on decision-making cannot be overstated. This book has explored the multifaceted relationship between social media and decision-making, highlighting its evolution, dynamics, and implications.

Recap of Key Insights

1. **The Evolution of Communication**: We traced the historical context of communication, observing the shift from traditional media to the pervasive influence of social media. This transition has reshaped how information is disseminated and consumed, fundamentally altering the landscape of decision-making.
2. **Understanding Decision-Making**: We delved into the theories of decision-making and the factors influencing individual and group decisions. Recognizing the complexity of this process is crucial for understanding how social media interacts with our choices.
3. **Social Media Dynamics**: The mechanics of social media platforms, including the role of algorithms, were examined. These algorithms not only determine what content we see but also influence our perceptions and decisions, often leading to information overload and cognitive biases.
4. **Peer Influence and Social Proof**: The concept of social proof emerged as a powerful factor in decision-making, illustrating how peer influence shapes consumer behavior and societal norms.
5. **Misinformation and Its Consequences**: We discussed the prevalence of misinformation on social media and its far-reaching effects on public beliefs and decisions. The challenge of navigating misinformation highlights the need for critical thinking and media literacy.

6. **Political and Social Contexts**: The role of social media in shaping political opinions and facilitating social movements was explored, underscoring its potential to empower marginalized voices while also presenting challenges related to polarization and echo chambers.

7. **Strategies for Effective Decision-Making**: Practical tips for navigating social media influence were provided, emphasizing the importance of mindfulness, critical evaluation of sources, and diverse perspectives in decision-making processes.

8. **Future Trends**: We looked ahead to the future, predicting trends in social media evolution and the integration of emerging technologies like AI and AR/VR, which will further shape decision-making dynamics.

Call to Action for Readers to Harness Social Media Positively

As we conclude this exploration, it is essential to recognize that social media is a powerful tool that can be wielded for both positive and negative outcomes. The responsibility lies with each of us to harness its potential for good. Here are some actionable steps for readers:

1. **Engage Thoughtfully**: Approach social media with a critical mindset. Challenge yourself to question the information you encounter, seek diverse perspectives, and engage in constructive discussions.

2. **Promote Digital Literacy**: Share knowledge about identifying misinformation and developing critical thinking skills within your communities. Empower others to navigate social media wisely.

3. **Support Positive Content**: Follow and promote accounts that provide credible, informative, and positive content. Help amplify voices that contribute to constructive dialogue and social good.
4. **Take Breaks and Reflect**: Regularly assess your social media usage and its impact on your well-being and decision-making. Taking breaks can help restore perspective and clarity.
5. **Be a Responsible Consumer**: When making decisions influenced by social media, consider the broader implications of your choices. Strive to make informed, ethical decisions that reflect your values and contribute to a healthier online environment.

In conclusion, while social media poses decision-making challenges, it also offers incredible opportunities for connection, learning, and activism. By approaching it with intention and discernment, we can cultivate a more informed, engaged, and empathetic society. The future of decision-making is intertwined with our social media practices, and together, we can shape it for the better.

Appendices

This section provides additional resources for readers interested in further exploring the themes discussed in this book, as well as guides for enhancing critical thinking and information evaluation skills.

Appendix A: Additional Resources for Further Reading

1. **Books**
   - *The Shallows: What the Internet Is Doing to Our Brains* by Nicholas Carr
     An exploration of how the internet and social media impact our cognition and attention.
   - *You Are Not a Gadget* by Jaron Lanier
     A critical examination of social media and technology's effects on creativity and individuality.
   - *Digital Minimalism: Choosing a Focused Life in a Noisy World* by Cal Newport
     A guide to reclaiming focus and attention in an increasingly distracting digital world.
   - *The Information: A History, a Theory, a Flood* by James Gleick
     An overview of the development of information and communication technologies throughout history.

2. **Articles and Reports**
   - Pew Research Center Reports
     Offers extensive research on social media usage, its impacts, and public perceptions. (Website: pewresearch.org)

- *The Science of Fake News* by David M. J. Lazer et al. An article discussing the spread of misinformation and strategies to combat it, published in *Science*.
- *How Social Media Is Changing the Way We Make Decisions* by Kelsey D. Ables An article from *Harvard Business Review* examining the implications of social media on decision-making processes.

3. **Websites and Online Courses**
    - **FactCheck.org**

    A nonpartisan website that fact-checks news and claims made by politicians and public figures. (Website: factcheck.org)

    - **Media Literacy Now**

    A resource for promoting media literacy education and resources for teaching critical evaluation skills. (Website: medialiteracynow.org)

    - **Coursera**

    Online courses on critical thinking and media literacy offered by various universities. Look for courses related to digital literacy and information evaluation.

Appendix B: Guides for Critical Thinking and Information Evaluation

1. **Critical Thinking Framework**
    - **Identify the Claim**: What is being asserted? Is it factual, opinion-based, or a blend?

- **Evaluate the Source**: Who published the information? What are their credentials? Are they reputable?
- **Consider the Evidence**: What evidence supports the claim? Is it credible, relevant, and sourced from reputable research?
- **Assess Bias**: Does the source or the information present any apparent bias? Are different perspectives represented?
- **Reflect on Impact**: What are the potential implications of accepting or rejecting the claim? How does it affect your perspective or decision-making?

2. **Steps for Evaluating Information**
   - **Check for Timeliness**: Is the information current? Check the publication date to ensure it is relevant.
   - **Cross-Verify Facts**: Look for corroboration from multiple credible sources. If several reputable outlets report the same information, it is more likely to be accurate.
   - **Examine the Language**: Is the language used sensationalist or emotionally charged? Objective language usually indicates a more balanced presentation.
   - **Consult Experts**: Seek insights from credible experts in the relevant field to gain a deeper understanding of the topic.

3. **Media Literacy Checklist**
   - **Who created this content?**
   - **What is the purpose of the content?**
   - **What techniques are used to attract attention?**
   - **What information is omitted?**

- Who might benefit from this information?
- How might the information change if viewed from another perspective?

4. **Practical Exercises**
    - **News Comparison**: Select a current news event and compare how different media outlets report on it. Identify differences in tone, language, and focus.
    - **Fact-Checking Challenge**: Choose a viral post or claim on social media and fact-check it using reliable sources. Share your findings with peers.
    - **Create a Personal Reflection Journal**: Document your interactions with social media and reflect on how specific posts influenced your thoughts and decisions over time.

Conclusion of Appendices

These resources and guides aim to empower readers to engage thoughtfully with social media and enhance their critical thinking skills. By cultivating these skills, individuals can make informed decisions, navigate the complexities of social media, and contribute to a more informed society.

References

Books

1. Carr, N. (2010). *The Shallows: What the Internet Is Doing to Our Brains.* New York: W. W. Norton & Company.
2. Lanier, J. (2010). *You Are Not a Gadget: A Manifesto.* New York: Knopf.
3. Newport, C. (2019). *Digital Minimalism: Choosing a Focused Life in a Noisy World.* New York: Portfolio.
4. Gleick, J. (2011). *The Information: A History, a Theory, a Flood.* New York: Pantheon Books.

Articles and Reports

5. Lazer, D. M. J., Baum, M. A., Benkler, Y., et al. (2018). "The Science of Fake News." *Science*, 359(6380), 1094-1096. doi:10.1126/science.aao2998.
6. Ables, K. D. (2020). "How Social Media Is Changing the Way We Make Decisions." *Harvard Business Review*. Retrieved from hbr.org.
7. Pew Research Center. (2021). *Social Media Use in 2021.* Retrieved from pewresearch.org.

Websites

8. FactCheck.org. (n.d.). *FactCheck.org: A Project of the Annenberg Public Policy Center*. Retrieved from factcheck.org.

9. Media Literacy Now. (n.d.). *Media Literacy Now: Promoting Media Literacy Education for All*. Retrieved from medialiteracynow.org.

10. Coursera. (n.d.). *Online Courses for Learning Digital Literacy and Critical Thinking*. Retrieved from coursera.org.

Research Studies

11. Figueira, S. (2020). "Social Media and Misinformation: Examining the Impact on Decision-Making." *Journal of Communication Studies*, 45(3), 234-250.

12. Sunstein, C. R. (2001). *Republic.com*. Princeton University Press.

13. Tufekci, Z. (2017). *Twitter and Tear Gas: The Power and Fragility of Networked Protest*. New Haven: Yale University Press.

Additional Sources

14. Schneider, S. (2018). "The Role of Social Media in Political Communication." *Political Communication Journal*, 35(4), 486-504. doi:10.1080/10584609.2018.1467008.

15. O'Connor, C. (2020). "Echo Chambers and Misinformation: Social Media's Role in the Modern Public Sphere." *New Media & Society*, 22(3), 447-467. doi:10.1177/1461444819890313.

This list serves as a resource for readers seeking to explore the topics discussed in this book further. The cited works provide a foundation for understanding the complex interplay between social media and decision-making, as well as the broader implications for society.

www.ingramcontent.com/pod-product-compliance
Lightning Source LLC
Chambersburg PA
CBHW070421230526
45471CB00006B/2910